A MIDSUMMER NIGHT'S DREAM

A MIDSUMMER NIGHT'S DREAM

By William Shakespeare

Adapted by Diana Stewart
Illustrated by Charles Shaw

RSVP
**RAINTREE
STECK-VAUGHN**
P U B L I S H E R S
The Steck-Vaughn Company

Austin, Texas

Library of Congress Number: 81-19272

Library of Congress Cataloging-in-Publication Data

Stewart, Diana.
  A midsummer night's dream.

  SUMMARY: An adaptation of the play in which fairy creatures meddle with varying results in the lives of humans wandering in the woods.
  [1. Fairies—Drama. 2. Plays]
  I. Shakespeare, William, 1564-1616. Midsummer night's dream. II. Shaw, Charles, ill. III. Title.
  PR2827.A25   1982   822.3'3   81-19272

ISBN 0-8172-1680-4 hardcover library binding

ISBN 0-8114-6833-X softcover binding

19 20 21 22 23 24 25   05 04

CAST OF CHARACTERS

Theseus — Duke of Athens
Egeus — Hermia's father
Lysander — in love with Hermia
Demetrius — in love with Hermia
Philostrate — Master of the Revels to Theseus

Hippolyta — Queen of the Amazons, betrothed to Theseus
Hermia — daughter of Egeus, in love with Lysander
Helena — in love with Demetrius

CLOWNS:
Quince — a carpenter
Snug — a joiner
Bottom — a weaver
Flute — a bellows mender
Snout — a tinker
Starveling — a tailor

Oberon — King of the Fairies
Titania — Queen of the Fairies
Puck — a mischievous spirit

FAIRIES:
Peaseblossom
Cobweb
Moth
Mustardseed

Other Fairies attending their King and Queen
Attendants on Theseus and Hippolyta

THE SETTING:
The scene is Athens and a wood nearby.

ACT I

Scene 1

The scene is in the palace of Theseus, the Duke of Athens. As a warrior, Theseus fought against the Amazons. He defeated them and brought Hippolyta, Queen of the Amazons, back to Athens with him. There he fell in love with her, and now they are to be married in four days' time. Theseus and Hippolyta enter.

THESEUS. Now, fair Hippolyta, our nuptial hour
    Draws near. Four happy days bring in
    Another moon. But, oh!
    How slow this old moon wanes!

HIPPOLYTA. Four days will quickly pass in night.
    Four nights will quickly dream away the time.

(*Egeus — a citizen of Athens — enters with his daughter Hermia. They are followed by Lysander — Hermia's love — and Demetrius, who wants to marry her.*)

EGEUS. Happy be Theseus, our renowned duke!

THESEUS. Thanks, good Egeus. What's the news with thee?

EGEUS. I come full of vexation! I come with
    Complaint against my child, my daughter Hermia.
    Come forth, Lysander! My gracious Duke,
    This man hath bewitched my child's heart.
    Thou, thou, Lysander! Thou hast given her rhymes,
    With cunning hast thou stolen my daughter's heart
    And turned her obedience — which is due to me! —
    To stubborn harshness.

    Come forth, Demetrius.
    (To Theseus)
    My noble lord,
    This man hath my consent to marry her.
    If she will not — here before Your Grace —
    Consent to marry Demetrius,
    I beg the ancient law of Athens:

6

As she is mine, I may dispose of her —
Either to this gentlemen Demetrius
Or to her death. So it is according to our law.

THESEUS. What say you, Hermia? Be advised, fair maid.
To you your father should be as a god.
And Demetrius is a worthy gentleman.

HERMIA. So is Lysander.

THESEUS. In himself he is.
But without your father's blessing,
The other must be held the worthier.

HERMIA. I beg Your Grace that I may know
The worst that may befall me
If I refuse to wed Demetrius.

THESEUS. Your choice is either to die or to leave
Forever the society of men.
If you do not yield to your father's choice,
You will don the dress of a nun,
Remain within the walls of a shady cloister,
And there live a barren sister all your life.

HERMIA. So will I grow, so live, so die, my lord,
Before I yield to Demetrius!

THESEUS. Take time to consider, Hermia!
By the next new moon —
The wedding day between my love and me —
Either prepare to die for
Disobedience to your father's will,
Or else to wed Demetrius,
As your father would have you
Or to take on the habit of the nun and
Embrace the single life.

DEMETRIUS. Relent, sweet Hermia! Lysander,
Yield to my certain rights!

LYSANDER. My lord, I am as well born as he
And as wealthy. My love is more than his.
And — which is more than all these boasts —
I am loved by the beauteous Hermia.

7

Demetrius made love to Nedar's daughter, Helena,
And won her soul. And she, sweet lady, dotes —
Devoutly dotes! — upon this spotted and inconstant
  man!

THESEUS. I must confess that I have heard this
And with Demetrius thought to speak.
But, being overfull of self-affairs,
I did forget.

But Demetrius, come.
And come, Egeus. You shall go with me.
I have some private words for you both.

(They exit, leaving Lysander and Hermia alone.)

LYSANDER. Ay me! For all I ever read
In tales or in history,
The course of true love never did run smooth.

HERMIA. If then true lovers have been ever crossed,
It stands as a rule of destiny.
Then let us learn patience,
Because it is a customary cross,
As much a part of love as thoughts and
Dreams and sighs, wishes and tears.

LYSANDER. I have a plan, Hermia. Therefore, hear me.
I have a widow aunt of great wealth.
She hath no child. From Athens is her
House remote seven leagues.
She respects me as her only son.
There, gentle Hermia, may I marry thee.
And to that place the sharp Athenian law
Cannot follow us.

If thou lovest me, then steal
Forth from thy father's house tomorrow night,
And in the wood outside the town — where
I did meet thee once with Helena —
There will I wait for thee.

HERMIA. My good Lysander!
I swear to thee by Cupid's strongest bow,
By his best arrow with the golden head,

8

By all the vows that ever men have broke —
In number more than ever women spoke —
In that same place thou has appointed me,
Tomorrow truly will I meet with thee!

(Helena enters.)

HELENA. You call me fair?
When it is your fair beauty Demetrius loves.
Your eyes are stars. Your tongue is sweet music.
Sickness is catching. O, were beauty so!
Oh, teach me how you look, and with what art
You sway the motion of Demetrius' heart!

HERMIA. I frown upon him, yet he loves me still.

HELENA. O that your frowns would teach my smiles such
skill.

HERMIA. I give him curses, yet he gives me love.

HELENA. O that my prayers could such affection move!

LYSANDER. Helena, we will unfold to you our plan.
Tomorrow night, when the moon will hide our flight,
We will steal away through the gates of Athens.

HERMIA. And in the wood — where often you and I
So often lay upon the primrose bed,
Emptying our hearts of their sweet secrets —
There my Lysander and myself shall meet,
To leave Athens forever.

Farewell, sweet playfellow. Pray for us!
And good luck grant thee thy Demetrius.

LYSANDER. Helena, adieu! As you on him,
May Demetrius dote on you!

*(They exit, leaving Helena to her own troubled thoughts.
She and Hermia have been friends all their lives. But now she
is jealous of Demetrius' love for her friend.)*

HELENA. Through Athens I am thought as fair as Hermia.
But what of that? Demetrius thinks not so.
Before Demetrius looked into Hermia's eyes,
He called down oaths that he was mine alone!

(She thinks of a plan. She will tell Demetrius that Lysander and Hermia plan to run away and marry.)

HELENA. I will go tell Demetrius of Hermia's flight.
Tomorrow night he will pursue her to the wood,
And for this piece of news, he will give me thanks.
And I will win him back again for my own.

Scene 2

The scene is at the house of Quince the carpenter. He has gathered a group of workers together to prepare a play for the duke's wedding party. They are all a bit foolish — clowns.

QUINCE. Marry, our play is: "The most lamentable comedy, and most cruel death of Pyramus and Thisby."

BOTTOM. A very good piece of work, I assure you, and a merry one. Now, good Peter Quince, call forth your actors by the scroll.

QUINCE. Answer as I call you. Nick Bottom, the weaver.

BOTTOM. Ready. Name what part I am for.

QUINCE. You, Nick Bottom, are set down for Pyramus. Francis Flute, the bellows mender.

FLUTE. Here, Peter Quince.

QUINCE. Flute, you must take Thisby on you.

FLUTE. What is Thisby? A wandering knight?

QUINCE. It is the lady that Pyramus must love.

BOTTOM. Let me play Thisby too. I'll speak in a monstrous little voice. (In a high, woman's voice) "Ah, Pyramus, my lover dear! Thy Thisby dear, and lady dear!"

QUINCE. No, no! You must play Pyramus. And you, Flute, Thisby.

BOTTOM. Well, proceed.

QUINCE. Robin Starveling, the tailor.

STARVELING. Here, Peter Quince.

QUINCE. Robin Starveling, you must play Thisby's mother. Tom Snout, the tinker.

SNOUT. Here Peter Quince.

QUINCE. You, Pyramus' father. Myself, Thisby's father. Snug, the joiner. You play the lion's part.

BOTTOM. Let me play the lion too. I will roar so that the duke will say: "Let him roar again. Let him roar again!"

QUINCE. You can play no part but Pyramus, Bottom. For Pyramus is a gentleman. Therefore, you must needs play Pyramus.

BOTTOM. Well, I will undertake it.

QUINCE. So, masters, here are your parts. I beg you to learn them by tomorrow night. We will meet in the wood, a mile outside of town — by moonlight. There we will rehearse. If we meet in the city, we shall be dogged with company, and our plans will be known. Tomorrow night, then. I pray you, fail me not.

BOTTOM. We will meet and there we may rehearse. Take pains, be prompt. Adieu!

(They exit.)

ACT II

Scene 1

The scene is in the wood outside of Athens the next night. A Fairy enters at one door and Puck at the other.

PUCK. How now, spirit! Whither wander you?

FAIRY. I do wander everywhere

To serve Titania — the Fairy Queen.
Farewell, you clumsy oaf of spirits.
I must be gone. Our queen and all her
Elves come here soon.

PUCK. The king doth keep his revels here tonight.
Take care he doth not see the queen.
Oberon is filled with anger
Because she has taken as her attendant
A lovely boy, stolen from an Indian king.
She never had so sweet a child,
And jealous Oberon would have the boy
To be a knight of his train.
But hark, Fairy! Here comes Oberon now!

FAIRY. And here comes my mistress. Would that he were
gone!

(*Oberon, King of Fairies, enters at one door with his train of fairies. At the other door enters Titania, his queen, with her attendants.*)

OBERON. Ill met by moonlight, proud Titania.

TITANIA. Why are thou here?
Why hast thou come from the far steep of India?
Already the fairy world is turned upside down
By our quarreling. The spring, the summer,
The fruitful autumn, and the angry winter change
Their usual dress. The bewildered world looks on
And knows not which is which.

OBERON. Amend it then. It is within thy power.
Why should Titania quarrel with her Oberon?
All I ask is the little boy to be my page.

TITANIA. Not if you gave me all the fairy land
Could you buy the child from me!
His mother was my friend,
And for her sake do I rear him up.
For her sake I will not part with him.

OBERON. How long within this wood intend you to stay?

TITANIA. Perhaps till after Theseus' wedding day.

If you will patiently dance with us
And see our moonlight revels, go with us,
If not, shun me, and I will avoid your haunts.

OBERON. Give me that boy, and I will go with thee.

TITANIA. Not for thy fairy kingdom. Fairies, away!
We shall quarrel if I longer stay.

(Titania exits with her train.)

OBERON. Well, go thy way!
(To himself)
Thou shalt not leave this wood
Till I have tormented thee for this injury.

My gentle Puck! Come hither!
Dost thou remember that once I sat upon a hill
And heard a mermaid on a dolphin's back
Singing so sweetly that the rude sea
Did grow quiet at her song,
And certain stars shot madly from their spheres,
To hear the sea maid's music?

PUCK. I remember.

OBERON. That very day I saw Cupid take aim
And shoot a golden arrow.
I marked the place where Cupid's bolt fell.
It fell upon a little flower.
Maidens call that flower love-in-idleness.

My gentle Puck, fetch me that flower,
The juice of it on sleeping eyelids
Will make the man or woman madly love
The next creature that it sees.

PUCK. I'll wing my way around the earth
In the twinkling of an eye!

(Puck exits to do his master's bidding, and Oberon makes his plans to punish Titania for refusing to give up the boy.)

OBERON. Having once this flower,
I'll watch Titania when she is asleep,
And drop the juice of it in her eyes.

The next thing she looks upon when waking —
Be it on lion, bear, or wolf, or bull,
Or meddling monkey, or on a busy ape —
She shall chase it with the soul of love.

And before I take this charm from off her sight —
As I can take it with another herb —
I'll make her give up her page to me.

(He hears the sound of someone coming.)

OBERON. But who comes here? I am invisible,
And I will overhear their conference.

(Demetrius enters. Helena is following him.)

DEMETRIUS. I love thee not! Therefore pursue me not.
Where is Lysander and fair Hermia?
The one I'll slay, the other slayeth me.
Thou told'st me they were stolen unto this wood.
Away! Get thee gone and follow me no more!

HELENA. You draw me — you hardhearted magnet —
But yet you draw not iron, for my heart
Is true as steel. Lose your power to draw,
And I shall have no power to follow you.

DEMETRIUS. Do not tempt my hatred.
I am sick when I do look on thee.

HELENA. And I am sick when I look not on you!

DEMETRIUS. You are sick indeed
To leave the city and commit yourself
Into the hands of one that loves you not,
To trust the opportunity of night in this deserted place
With your innocence.

HELENA. It is not night when I do see your face,
Therefore I think I am not in the night.
Nor doth this wood lack worlds of company,
For you in my eyes are all the world.
Then how can it be said I am alone,
When all the world is here to look on me?

DEMETRIUS. Let me go!

Or if thou follow me, do not believe
But I shall do thee mischief in the wood.

(Demetrius exits.)

HELENA. I'll follow thee, and make a heaven of hell.
I'll die by the hand I love so well.

(Helena exits. Oberon — invisible to the two mortals — has seen and heard everything Demetrius and Helena have said. He feels sorry for Helena.)

OBERON. Fare thee well, girl.
Before he do leave this wood,
Thou shalt fly from him,
And he shall seek thy love.

(Puck re-enters with the flower.)

OBERON. Hast thou the flower there?

PUCK. Ay, there it is.

OBERON. I pray thee, give it to me.
I know a bank where the wild thyme grows,
There sometime Titania sleeps of a night.
(He takes the magic flower from Puck.)
And with the juice of this, I'll streak her eyes,
And make her full of hateful dreams.
Take thou some of the flower.
Seek through this grove.
A sweet Athenian lady is in love
With a disdainful youth.
Rub the juice in his eyes.
But do it when the next thing he sees
May be the lady. Thou shalt know the man
By the Athenian clothes he hath on.
And see that thou meet me
Before the first cock crow.

PUCK. Fear not, my lord. Your servant shall do so.

(They exit.)

Scene 2

The scene is in another part of the woods. Titania enters with her train of fairies.

TITANIA. Come! A dance and a fairy song.
Sing me now to sleep, and
Then to your duties and let me rest.

(The fairies dance and sing. Titania falls asleep, and the fairies exit. Oberon enters looking for Titania. He sees her sleeping and goes to her. Carefully he squeezes the juice from the magic flower on her eyelids.)

OBERON. What thou seest when thou dost wake,
Do it for thy true love take;
Love and languish for his sake.
Be it lynx or cat or bear,
Leopard or boar with bristled hair,
In thy eye that shall appear
When thou wakest, it is thy dear.
Wake when some vile thing is near!

(Oberon exits and Lysander and Hermia enter from the other side.)

LYSANDER. Fair love, you faint with wandering in the wood.
And to speak the truth, I have lost our way.
We'll rest here, Hermia, if you think it good.
And wait for the comfort of the day.

HERMIA. Be it so, Lysander. Find you a bed,
And upon this bank I will rest my head.

(They lie down a way apart and fall asleep. Puck enters.)

PUCK. Who is here?
He does wear the clothes of Athens!
This is he, my master says,
That despises the Athenian maid.
And here the maiden sleeps
On the dank and dirty ground.

21

Pretty soul!
(He takes the flower and squeezes the juice on Lysander's eyelids.)
Upon his eyes I throw
All the power of this charm.
So awake when I am gone,
For I must now to Oberon.

(He exits. Demetrius and Helena enter — running.)

HELENA. Oh, wilt thou leave me in the dark?
Do not so!

DEMETRIUS. I go alone!

(He exits. Helena is too tired to follow any longer.)

HELENA. O, I am out of breath!

(Suddenly she sees Lysander asleep still on the ground.)

HELENA. But who is here? Lysander! On the ground!
Dead? Or asleep? I see no blood, no wound.
Lysander, if you live, good sir, awake!

(Lysander awakes and Puck's magic flower works its spell. Lysander is instantly in love with Helena — the first woman he sees when he opens his eyes.)

LYSANDER. Ah, I am awake, Helena, and would run
Through fire for your sweet sake.
Where is Demetrius? I shall find him
And he shall perish on my sword!

HELENA. Do not say so, Lysander. Though he
Love your Hermia, yet Hermia still loves you!
Be content!

LYSANDER. Content with Hermia? No, I do repent
Every tedious minute I have spent with her.
I love not Hermia but Helena.
Who would not change a raven for a dove?

HELENA. Why do you mock me, sir?
What have I done to deserve your scorn?
O, that a lady, of one man refused,
Should of another therefore be abused!

23

(She exits.)

LYSANDER. She did not see Hermia.
Hermia, sleep thou there,
And never again come near Lysander.

(Lysander exits. Hermia awakens from a nightmare.)

HERMIA. Ay me, for pity! What a dream was that!
Lysander, look how I do shake with fear.
I thought a serpent was eating my heart away
And you sat smiling at his cruel feast.
(She sees that Lysander is gone.)
Lysander! Lysander! Lord!
What, out of hearing? Gone? No sound? No word?
Alack, where are you? Speak if you can hear.
Speak, I nearly swoon with fear!
(She listens and hears nothing.)
No? Then I see you are not here.
Either death or you I'll find immediately.

(She exits.)

ACT III

Scene 1

The scene is in the part of the woods where Titania lies sleeping. The clowns — Quince, Snug, Bottom, Flute, Snout, and Starveling — enter.

BOTTOM. We are all met.

QUINCE. And here's a place for our rehearsal. This green plot shall be our stage. We will do it in action as we will before the Duke.

There are two hard things. First, how to bring moonlight into a room. For, you know, Pyramus and Thisby meet by moonlight.

BOTTOM. One of us must come in with a lantern and say he comes in the person of Moonshine.

QUINCE. Ay! Then there is another thing. We must have a wall in the room. Pyramus and Thisby — says the story — did talk through the chink of a wall.

BOTTOM. Some man or other must be Wall. And let him have some plaster about him. Let him hold his fingers thus, and through that crack shall Pyramus and Thisby whisper.

QUINCE. Then all is well. Come, sit down, every mother's son, and rehearse your parts. Pyramus, you begin. When you have spoken your speech, enter into that thicket of bushes.

(Puck enters, invisible to the clowns.)

PUCK. What clownish fools are these
So near where the Fairy Queen sleeps?
What? Do they rehearse a play?
Be a listener and an actor too perhaps.

QUINCE. Speak, Pyramus. Thisby, come forth.

PYRAMUS (BOTTOM). Thisby, the flowers of odious savors sweet—

QUINCE. Odors, odors!

PYRAMUS. — odors savors sweet:
So hath thy breath, my dearest Thisby dear.
But hark, a voice! Stay thou but here awhile,
And by and by I will to thee appear.

(He exits into the bushes.)

PUCK. A stranger Pyramus than I have ever seen!

(Puck follows Bottom into the bushes.)

THISBY. Most radiant Pyramus, most lily-white of hue.
O — as true as truest horse, that yet would never tire.

(This is Bottom's cue to re-enter. But while he has been waiting in the bushes, Puck has changed his head to the head of an ass. Puck and Bottom enter.)

PYRAMUS (BOTTOM). If I were fair, Thisby, I were only thine.

(His friends take one look at him and are horrified. He, however, doesn't know what has happened.)

QUINCE. O monstrous! O strange! We are haunted. Pray, friends! Fly! Help!

(All the clowns exit leaving a bewildered Bottom.)

PUCK. *(Following after the clowns — unseen and unheard.)*
I'll follow you. I'll lead you a merry round
Through bogs, through bush, through brier.

(He exits.)

BOTTOM. I see their mischief! This is to make an ass of me — to frighten me. But I will not stir from this place. I will walk up and down here and sing. Then they shall hear me and see I am not afraid.

(He begins to sing in a loud voice. The song is so loud that it awakens Titania sleeping nearby. She is caught by the magic spell of the flower juice Oberon has put on her eyelids. Bottom is her new love.)

TITANIA. What angel wakes me from my flowery bed?
I pray thee, gentle mortal, sing again!
My ear is thrilled by thy voice.
Mine eye is enthralled by thy shape.
The force of thy fair virtue doth move me
On the first view to say — to swear! I love thee!

BOTTOM. Methinks, mistress, you should have little reason for that. And yet, to say the truth, reason and love keep little company together nowadays.

TITANIA. Thou art as wise as thou art beautiful.

BOTTOM. Not so, I am afraid. But if I have wit enough to get out of this wood, I have enough to serve me.

TITANIA. Do not desire to go out of this wood.
Thou shalt remain here, whether thou wilt or not.
I do love thee. Therefore, go with me.
I'll give thee fairies to attend on thee.
(She calls her fairies to come forth.)
Peaseblossom! Cobweb! Moth! And Mustardseed!

(The four fairies enter.)

TITANIA. Be kind and courteous to this gentleman.
Nod to him, elves, and serve him well.

(Titania exits with Bottom and the fairies.)

Scene 2

The scene is in another part of the wood. Oberon enters.

OBERON. I wonder if Titania be awaked.
Then, what it was that next came in her eye
Which she must love to foolishness.

(Puck enters.)

OBERON. Here comes my messenger. How now, Puck?

PUCK. My mistress is in love with a monster!
Near to her flowery bed a crew of fools
Were met together to rehearse a play
For great Theseus' wedding revelries.
The biggest clown of them all
Who represented Pyramus in their play
Left the scene and entered the bushes.
There did I fix upon him an ass's head.
When his fellow clowns did spy him,
They did fly from the sight of him.
I led them on in this distracted fear,
And left sweet Pyramus transformed there.
When in that moment, so it came to pass,
Titania waked and straightway loved an ass!

OBERON. This is better than I could have planned!
But has thou yet sprinkled the Athenian's eyes
With the love juice, as I did bid thee do?

PUCK. That is finished too. I took him sleeping,
With the Athenian woman by his side,
That when he waked, she must be seen.

29

(Demetrius and Hermia enter. They cannot see Oberon and Puck standing there.)

OBERON. This is the same Athenian.

PUCK. This is the woman, but this is not the man!

HERMIA. If thou hast slain Lysander in his sleep
Plunge in thy dagger and kill me too!
The sun was not so true as he to me.

DEMETRIUS. I am not guilty of Lysander's death.
Nor is he dead, for all that I know.

HERMIA. I pray thee, tell me then that he is well.

DEMETRIUS. And if I could, what should I get in return?

HERMIA. A gift: never to see me more!
And from thy hated presence part I so.
See me no more, whether he be dead or no.

(Hermia exits.)

DEMETRIUS. There is no following her in this fierce mood.
I will remain here for a while.

(Demetrius lies down and falls asleep. Oberon sees at once that Puck has made a mistake. He has put the love juice on the eyelids of the wrong man.)

OBERON. What hast thou done?
Hast thou laid the love juice on some truelove's sight?
About the wood go swifter than the wind
And look to find Helena of Athens.
By some illusion see thou bring her here.

(Puck exits to find Helena. Oberon goes to the sleeping Demetrius and rubs the magic love juice on his eyelids. Puck re-enters.)

PUCK. Captain of our fairy band,
Helena is here at hand;
And the youth, mistook by me,
Pleading for a lover's fee.
Lord, what fools these mortals be!

OBERON. Stand aside. The noise they make
　　Will cause Demetrius to awake.

PUCK. Then will two at once woo one!
　　That must needs be sport alone.

(Lysander and Helena enter — arguing. Helena still believes that he is making fun of her, that he is pretending to love her to scorn her.)

LYSANDER. Why should you think that I should woo in
　　scorn?
　　Scorn and derision never come in tears.
　　Look! When I vow, I weep!

HELENA. These vows are Hermia's! Will you give her over?

LYSANDER. I had no judgment when I swore to her.

HELENA. Nor none, in my mind, now you give her over.

(Their arguing has awakened Demetrius. He sees Helena and falls under the spell. Instantly he loves her.)

DEMETRIUS. O Helena! Goddess, nymph, perfect, divine!
　　To what, my love, shall I compare thine eyes?
　　Oh, let me kiss this princess of pure white!
　　This seal of bliss!

HELENA. O spite! O hell! I see you all are bent
　　On using me for your merriment.
　　If you were gentlemen,
　　You would not do me this injury.

LYSANDER. You are unkind, Demetrius, for you love
　　Hermia.
　　And here — with all good will, with all my heart —
　　I yield Hermia's love to you. It is Helena here
　　That I do love, and will do till my death.

DEMETRIUS. Lysander, keep thy Hermia.
　　If ever I loved her, all that love is gone.
　　My heart has returned to Helena, there to remain.
　　Look! Yonder comes thy love Hermia.

(Hermia enters. She has heard Lysander speaking and followed the sound of his voice.)

HERMIA. (To Lysander)
Why unkindly didst thou leave me so?

LYSANDER. Why should I stay, when love did press me to go?

HERMIA. What love could press Lysander from my side?

LYSANDER. Lysander's love for the fair Helena.
Why seekest thou me? Could you not see
The hate I bare thee made me leave thee so?

HERMIA. It cannot be!

HELENA. Lo, Hermia is part of this plot!
Hermia! Most ungrateful maid!
O, is all forgot?
All school days' friendship?
And will you tear our childhood love apart
To join with men in scorning your poor friend?

HERMIA. I am amazed at your passionate words.
I scorn you not. It seems that you scorn me.

HELENA. Have you not set Lysander — in scorn! —
To follow me and praise my eyes and face?
And made your other love, Demetrius,
To call me goddess, nymph, divine and rare?
Why else speaks he this way to her he hates?
And why else doth Lysander deny his love for you?

(She starts to leave, but Lysander stops her.)

LYSANDER. Stay, gentle Helena!
My love, my life, my soul, fair Helena!

HERMIA. Sweet, do not scorn her so.

LYSANDER. (Ignoring Hermia)
Helena, I love thee!

DEMETRIUS. I say I love thee more than he can do.

HERMIA. Lysander! What change is this, sweet love?

LYSANDER. Thy love? Out, hated medicine!
O hated poison! Away!

HERMIA. Hated? O, me! Why, my love?
Am I not Hermia? Are not you Lysander?

LYSANDER. And I never desire to see thee more!
I do hate thee and love Helena.

HERMIA. (To Helena)
You thief of love! What, have you come by night
And stolen my love's heart from him?
(To Lysander and Demetrius)
Now I see that she has compared our size!
She hath urged her height — her tall form!
(To Helena)
Are you grown so high in my love's eyes
Because I am so small and so low?
How low am I — thou painted maypole!
How low am I? I am not yet so low
That my nails cannot reach unto thine eyes
To scratch them out!

LYSANDER. (To Hermia) Get you gone, you dwarf!
Demetrius, follow me — if thou darest! And
We will see who has the right to the love
Of the fair Helena!

*(Lysander and Demetrius exit to fight for the love of Helena.
Helena starts to leave, but Hermia stops her.)*

HERMIA. Nay, do not leave. This coil is all your fault!

HELENA. I will no longer stay in your curst company.
Your hands may be quicker for a fray,
My legs are longer, though, to run away!

(Helena turns and runs out with Hermia close behind her.)

OBERON. Puck, didst thou commit this mischief willfully?

PUCK. Believe me, O king! A mistake!
Did you not tell me I should know the man
By the Athenian clothes he had on?

OBERON. Well, thou see'st these lovers seek a place to fight.

Go, therefore, Puck, and cover the night with a black
   fog.
From each other see that thou leadest them away.
Til exhausted they fall asleep.

Then crush this herb into Lysander's eye.
When next he wakes this whole affair
Shall seem a dream — the magic spell broken.

*(Oberon exits. Puck goes about his master's business. One
by one he leads Demetrius and Lysander on a chase through
the black woods until they fall asleep. Helena enters. She
does not see the two men sleeping on the ground.)*

HELENA. O weary night. O long and tedious night!

*(She, too, falls asleep as Puck watches on. He looks at the
three mortals sleeping.)*

PUCK. Only three? Come one more.
Two of both kinds makes up four.

*(Hermia enters. She has been wandering lost through the
woods.)*

HERMIA. My legs can keep no pace with my desires.
Here will I rest me till the break of day.

*(She lies down and goes to sleep. Puck takes the herb that will
undo the spell and squeezes the juice on Lysander's eyes.)*

PUCK. On the ground
Sleep sound.
I'll apply
To your eye,
Gentle lover, remedy.

ACT IV

Scene 1

The scene is the part of the woods where Lysander,
Demetrius, Helena, and Hermia lie sleeping. Titania en-

ters with Bottom. He still has the ass's head. They are followed by Titania's fairies. Oberon is behind them, out of sight.

TITANIA. (To Bottom)
　　Come, sit thee down upon this flowery bed,
　　And let me caress your fair cheeks,
　　Stick roses in thy sleek, smooth head,
　　And kiss thy lovely large ears.
　　Sleep thou, and I will wind thee in my arms.
　　Fairies, be gone!

　　(Titania and Bottom fall asleep in each other's arms. Puck enters and goes to Oberon — who has been watching his queen and the fool.)

OBERON. Welcome, good Puck.
　　See'st thou this sight?
　　Now I do begin to pity her.

　　A short while ago I met her in the wood
　　Seeking flowers for this hateful fool.
　　Then I did ask of her her beloved child
　　Which straight she gave me.
　　And now I have the boy, I will undo
　　This hateful spell on her eyes.

　　And, gentle Puck, take the ass's head
　　From off this Athenian clown so
　　That when he awakens with all the rest
　　He may to Athens again return
　　And think no more of this night's events.
　　But consider it nothing more than a dream.

　　(He squeezes the healing herb on Titania's eyes.)

OBERON. (To the queen)
　　Be as thou wast wont to be.
　　See as thou wast wont to see!

TITANIA. My Oberon, what visions have I seen!
　　I thought I was in love with an ass.

OBERON. There lies your love.

TITANIA. How came these things to pass?
O, how mine eyes do loathe his face now!

OBERON. Puck, take off this head!
Titania, music call!

(Titania and Oberon dance. Their quarrels are over. Once again they are reunited as lovers. Puck interrupts them.)

PUCK. Fairy King, attend, and mark!
I do hear the morning lark.

(The fairies must return to fairy land before daylight. They exit.)

(A horn sounds. Theseus, Hippolyta, and Egeus enter with the Duke's attendants. They come upon the four lovers and Bottom asleep on the ground.)

THESEUS. Huntsman, wake them with thy horns.

(The horns sound and the four lovers awake.)

THESEUS. I pray you all, stand up.
How came you here?

LYSANDER. My lord, I cannot truly say how I came here.
But I think — for truly would I speak —
I came with Hermia hither. Our intent
Was to be gone from Athens, away from
The danger of the Athenian law —

EGEUS. Enough, enough, my lord. You have enough.
I beg the law upon his head.
They would have stolen away. They would,
Demetrius, have robbed you of your wife
And me of my consent.

DEMETRIUS. My lord, fair Helena told me of their plan.
And I in a fury hither followed them.
Fair Helena followed me out of love.

My good lord, I know not by what power,
But my love for Hermia melted as the snow.
Now the object and the pleasure of mine eye

Is only Helena. To her, my lord,
Was I betrothed before I saw Hermia.
But, like one who is sick, did I loathe this food.
But now in health, I come to my natural taste.

THESEUS. Egeus, I will overbear your will.
In the temple, by and by, with us
These couples shall eternally be knit.
(To the young lovers)
Away with us to Athens!
Come, Hippolyta.

(They exit and Bottom awakens.)

BOTTOM. Heigh-ho! Peter Quince? Flute? Snout? Starveling? What? Stolen away and left me asleep? I have
had a dream, past the wit of man to say what dream it
was. Man is but an ass, if he goes about telling this
dream! I will get Peter Quince to write a poem of it. It
shall be called "Bottom's Dream" because it hath no
bottom. And I will sing it in the latter end of a play
before the Duke.

(He exits.)

ACT V
Scene 1

The scene is in Theseus' palace in Athens. The mar-
riages of Theseus and Hippolyta, Lysander and Hermia,
and Demetrius and Helena have all taken place. The wedding feast is over and now the company has gathered.

THESEUS. (To the young lovers)
Joy, gentle friends! Joy and fresh days of love
Accompany your hearts!
What revels are in hand? Is there no play?
Call Philostrate.

*(Philostrate — Master of Revels to Theseus — comes
forward.)*

PHILOSTRATE. Here, mighty Theseus.

THESEUS. Say, what have you for this evening?
   What dance? What music? How shall we beguile
   The lazy time if not with some delight?

PHILOSTRATE. Here is a list of those that are ready.
   Make choice of which your Highness will see first.

   *(He gives Theseus a paper to look over. Theseus dismisses
   some and then comes to the clowns' play.)*

THESEUS. (Reading) "A tedious brief scene of young
   Pyramus
   And his love Thisby; very tragical mirth."
   Merry and tragical? Tedious and brief?
   That is hot ice and very strange snow.
   Who are they that do perform it?

PHILOSTRATE. Hard-working men of Athens,
   Who have never labored with their minds till now.

THESEUS. We will hear it!

PHILOSTRATE. No, my noble lord.
   It is not for you. I have heard it!

   *(Theseus, however, is touched that some of his simple, hard-
   working Athenians have prepared a play to help celebrate his
   wedding.)*

THESEUS. I will hear that play.
   For never anything can be amiss,
   When simpleness and duty tender it.
   Go, bring them in. Take your places, ladies.

   *(Philostrate leaves to find Quince, Bottom and the rest of the
   players. They enter and take their places. Snout — covered
   with mud — limestone — is the Wall. He begins the play.)*

WALL. In this same play it doth befall.
   That I — one Snout by name — represent a wall.
   And such a wall, as I would have you think,
   That had in it a hole or chink,
   Through which the lovers, Pyramus and Thisby,
   Did whisper often very secretly.

(He parts his fingers to make the chink.)

PYRAMUS (BOTTOM). O grim night! O night so black.
    O night, O night! Alack, alack, alack.

    And thou, O wall, O sweet, O lovely wall,
    That stand'st between her father's ground and mine.
    Show me thy chink, to blink through with mine eyes!

(The Wall holds his fingers open. Thisby enters on the other side of the Wall.)

THISBY. O wall, often has thou heard my moans.
    For parting my fair Pyramus and me!

PYRAMUS. I see a voice! Now will I to the chink,
    To see if I can hear my Thisby's face.

THISBY. Thou art my love, I think.

PYRAMUS. Wilt thou meet me straightway at Ninny's tomb?

THISBY. I come without delay.

(Pyramus and Thisby exit.)

WALL. Thus have I, Wall, played my part so.
    And being done, this wall doth go.

(The Wall exits.)

HIPPOLYTA. This is the silliest stuff that ever I heard!

THESEUS. If we think no worse of them than they think of
    themselves, they are excellent men. Look! Here come
    two noble beasts in — a man and a lion.

(Snug enters as the Lion and Starveling enters as Moonshine.)

LION. You ladies, whose gentle hearts do fear
    The smallest mouse that creeps on the floor,
    You may perhaps both quake and tremble here,
    When lion rough in wildest rage doth roar.

    Then know that I am Snug the joiner,
    No fierce lion.

MOONSHINE. This lantern doth the moon represent.
And myself am the man in the moon.

(Thisby enters.)

THISBY. This is old Ninny's tomb. Where is my love?

(The lion roars and Thisby runs away.)

DEMETRIUS. Well roared, Lion.

THESEUS. Well run, Thisby.

HIPPOLYTA. Well shone, Moon.

(Thisby has dropped her cloak and left it behind. The Lion picks it up in his bloody mouth and then drops it and exits. Pyramus enters.)

PYRAMUS. Sweet Moon, I thank thee for thy light.
I thank thee, Moon, for shining now so bright.

(Suddenly he sees Thisby's cloak lying on the ground all covered with blood. He believes that the lion has eaten his love.)

PYRAMUS. What dreadful sight is here!
Eyes, do you see? My love's cloak,
Stained with blood!

Come, tears!
Out, sword!
(He stabs himself.)
Thus I die. Thus, thus, thus.
Now I am dead.
Now I die, die, die, die, die.
(He dies.)

THESEUS. Here comes Thisby, and her passionate speech ends the play.

HIPPOLYTA. Methinks she should not use a long one for such a Pyramus. I hope she will be brief.

(Thisby enters and sees Pyramus lying on the ground.)

THISBY. Asleep, my love?

What, dead, my dove?
O Pyramus, arise!
Speak, speak!
Dead, dead!
(She takes Pyramus' sword.)
Come, trusty sword,
Come, blade, my breast!
(She stabs herself.)
And farewell, friends.
Thus Thisby ends.
(She dies.)

THESEUS. Moonshine and Lion are left to bury the dead.

DEMETRIUS. Ay, and Wall too.

BOTTOM. (Sitting up)
No, I assure you. Will it please you to see the epilogue?

THESEUS. No epilogue, I pray you.
It was a fine tragedy and very well played.
Let your epilogue alone.

But come! Lovers, to bed. It is almost fairy time.
This play hath well beguiled
The heavy gait of night. Sweet friends, to bed.

(The entire group exits, leaving the great hall silent. Puck enters.)

PUCK. If we shadows have offended,
Think but this, and all is mended:
Think that you have slumbered here
While these visions did appear.

(He exits.)

GLOSSARY

amorous (am′ ə rəs)   easily falling in love

beguile (bi gīl′)   to spend time doing something pleasant

cloister (kloi′ stər)   a place where people spend their lives devoted to a religion

disdainful (dis dān′ fəl)   full of pride and scorn

enthrall (in throl′)   to hold by a spell or by slavery

inconstant (in kan′ stənt)   likely to change often without good reason

joiner (joi′ nər)   a person whose work is making things from pieces of wood

reveling (rev′ əl ing)   a wild party or celebration

transform (trans form′)   to change shape

vexation (vek sā′ shən)   the state of being troubled or distressed